THE TEACHER

WITHIN

Recognizing the Best in Children

Nelda C. Toothman

Order this book online at www.trafford.com
or email orders@trafford.com

Most Trafford titles are also available at major online book retailers.

Print information available on the last page.

ISBN: 978-1-5536-9750-3 (sc)
ISBN: 978-1-4122-4917-1 (e)

Trafford rev. 03/09/2023

 www.trafford.com

North America & international
toll-free: 844-688-6899 (USA & Canada)
fax: 812 355 4082

GRATIFICATIONS

To my husband Rex, whose love and tireless assistance helped to bring my words to these pages.

To my actor friend, Barbara Bates Smith, who so generously committed her time in transferring my stories from tape to the printed word.

To my friend and fellow educator colleague, Marilyn Katzenmeyer, who wrote my Foreword, helped me structure my thoughts and facilitated a very helpful feedback session with fellow educators and friends.

To my writing coach, Jim Ballard, who was my kind and understanding mentor and editor throughout.

TABLE OF CONTENTS

I have come to a frightening conclusion.
I am the decisive element in the
classroom.
It is my personal approach that creates
the climate.
It is my daily mood that makes the
weather.
As a teacher I possess tremendous
power to make a child's life miserable
or joyous.
I can be a tool of torture or an
instrument of inspiration.
I can humiliate or humor, hurt or heal.
In all situations, it is my response that
decides whether a crisis
Will be escalated or de-escalated, and a
child humanized or de-humanized.

Haim Ginott
Between Teacher and Child

FOREWORD

If you are like me, you find yourself looking back on "the good old days," yearning for simpler times. You feel challenged to understand the forces of destruction that have violated our country. You grieve for the peacefulness that seems suddenly to have been snatched away from life as we knew it. And you wonder how you can make an impact in a world that seems seriously out of control. Even in such disturbing times there can come desperately needed rays of hope to remind us of the importance of caring for every precious human being we encounter. Surely one of these blessings is Nelda Toothman's *The Teacher Within: Recognizing the Best in Children.*

Those of us who became educators entered this field to make a difference in the lives of children. Given today's context, many of us have come to question the very possibility of doing so. Over the past decade the media have characterized the Nation's schools as seriously declining environments: reports of bullying, racial tensions, and escalating violence have become commonplace. Most teachers trying to do their jobs despite these trends must battle another growing distraction: the high stakes test mania. There is increasing top-down pressure for performance--the state threatens the district office personnel, who in turn pressure the principals, who pressure the teachers, who transmit the stress to students. Given these strains, increasing numbers of teachers grow dissatisfied with their lack of autonomy and creativity and move to change careers. Also, more talented and effective school principals forsake their leadership roles through early retirements, and there are fewer candidates seeking these administrative positions.

These are times when growing children must learn how to be resilient—how to emerge from the very dangers, setbacks and uncertainties that tend to cripple others, to lead healthy and productive lives. Studies of such resilient children have shown that the most important factor in nearly every case was a supportive one-on-one relationship with a caring adult. What can we do when by and large students across our country are not experiencing the care, attention and nurturing that school personnel wish they could be providing? One answer is to learn from a master, to study how such life-strengthening support was supplied magnificently in the past.

Nelda Toothman is one of those extraordinarily gifted influencers. Each of her simple, compelling stories illustrates a particular principle of effective teaching. Reading her self-searching analysis of why each intervention worked, we are reminded that positively impacting others is not a trick, but a commitment to bringing out their best. We ponder how we can refashion our own stories of influencing those we work with and care about.

The Teacher Within comes just in time to touch our complex and troubling days with its refreshing ray of hope. It should be required reading for all of us who need to get back in touch with our prime reasons for being. Whether we are teachers, managers, coaches or parents, Nelda Toothman's introspection motivates us to rethink our own lives and behaviors, to analyze how we will respond to the

challenges we face individually, in our homes, in our

classrooms and in our nation.

Dr. Marilyn Katzenmeyer
Teacher, Educational Consultant, Co-author, *Awakening the Sleeping Giant: Helping Teachers Develop as Leaders*, 2nd Edition, Thousand Oaks, CA: Corwin Press, 2001

INTRODUCTION

We all arrive on the planet with some sort of design or purpose. Being a teacher was my purpose. In my career as a teacher, I became the biggest learner. I did not learn facts or content, but I learned about how to relate to children and adults. There was something I had that truly worked with children. Later I learned that it also worked with adults. Now that I am eighty, I'm wondering, "Why was teaching so easy for me? Did I come into the world with a stamp on me that said, 'This person can teach?' Did my label say, 'This person can help children. She can make a difference.'" I wonder...

In 1969 when I was an undergraduate student at Florida State University, I took a class with a wonderful math education professor. Later when I was applying for a teaching position, I asked him to write a recommendation for me. Among other things he wrote, "Nelda knows how to teach like nobody ever taught her." What that professor predicted about me, in succeeding years proved true. I don't say that to brag – or even to take credit for it. Frankly, why I've been fortunate enough to do what I came into the world to do is still a mystery to me.

Not everybody should be a teacher. It doesn't require any particular brilliance to know how to treat a child, but some of my colleagues seemed not to get it. It amazed me, when I was teaching, to hear teachers express their frustration: "These kids are driving me nuts!" Some teachers seemed to vent their anger and complain about all the things that were wrong in their classrooms. I never felt that way. I almost never heard these teachers say how excited they were about being at school or about what they were going to do with the students that day. They focused on what was wrong rather than what was right. That "ain't-it-awful" game they played in the teachers' lounge just made me glad that I felt differently. The two things that I really experienced in teaching were joy and success.

Teaching does take considerable thought, but more importantly it takes respect for the students we teach. If we want to reach children, we have to be willing to be on the same human-being level as they are. Take for example David, a fourth-grade boy (who is now a doctor in Winter Haven, Florida) who never listened to all the things I told him to do. He was no trouble, but he had his own way of learning and participating in my class. He didn't work on the math problems I put on the board for all the students to do or write the sentences I asked him to write. I could have insisted he do things my way. I knew at some level that I should let him progress at his speed and in his way. In a recent conversation he recalled, "You used to let me read under the table when I was in your class instead of in the chair." Once his father commented at a parent-teacher conference with me, "I just want to tell you I don't know how you have done so well with David. I want to compliment you on the success you've had with my son." I smiled and answered, "I learned the very first day that David was smarter than I was."

A friend of mine and a retired teacher educator once had me listen to an audio tape on which the speaker said, "Teachers need to own their classrooms." I bristled at that idea at first, but later I came to agree with it. When I was training teachers, I talked about the idea this way: "You own your own home, but when guests arrive you treat them with respect."

The same is true with the ways we treat children in our classrooms. Teachers do need to work out ways of "owning" the classroom. They also need to allow their students to partner with them in that effort. Amazing results can occur when you "co-own" a classroom with children.

When a teacher's relationship with the students is positive, most of the time can be spent in this partnership. When things get out of sync in a classroom, as they are bound to do sometimes, the teacher must be able to bring out her most assertive self. The teacher must bring an end to whatever is disturbing or upsetting the classroom. Somehow, I have always found this easy to do. I'm not a very big person, and I'm not very loud. My success with classroom control had to do with something inside of me--

my gut or intuition, some might call it. I learned that when I behaved in a certain way, students would cooperate.

The "something inside me" is what this book is about. Instead of preaching about how to teach, how to manage students or how to get respect, I want to assist readers to concentrate on what's inside them. I know what it is inside of me that resulted in success, but I don't know how to tell what it is for you. That's why I am telling my teaching stories. That "something" is found in my stories. I share my experiences with the hope that others may find their own "something inside" that works for children.

In this book I will share stories that I believe will speak to others about the importance of relationships. In one sense this book is about how fortunate I have been in my life without ever having a plan in mind. I have selected stories that taught me, touched my heart and gave me a marvelous life for the last forty-plus years of working with children and teachers. The stories emphasize concepts that I believe are important to the relationships teachers can build with their students.

It is not my intention for the section on Nelda to be an autobiography, but as I was writing this book and sharing my draft with others, they encouraged me to include stories about my early life and how it shaped me to be the teacher and person I became. I have learned much in my life from metaphors. Some of these metaphors, such as the little "seamster" of Mrs. Coomer's naming and the new ground on my father's farm, will surface as you read my book. The stories are intended to illustrate, for people who influence others, a central principle: rather than trying to fix people or change them, relate to them and love them. The students in these stories have helped me to live, to think and to become. My hope is that readers of the stories will be led to reflect on their own unique stories, the stories of fulfillment that lie within each of them.

STORIES ABOUT TEACHING

Then said a teacher, speak to us of teaching. And he said:
No man can reveal to you aught but that which already lies asleep in the dawning of your knowledge.
If he is indeed wise he does not bid you enter the house of his wisdom, but rather leads you to the threshold of your own mind.
For the vision of one man lends not its wings to another man.

-- Kahlil Gibran

GIRL SCOUTS

*Each second we live is a new and unique
moment of the universe; a moment that never was
before and never will be again. And what do we
teach our children in school? We teach them that
two and two make four and that Paris is the capital
of France. When will we also teach them what they
are? We should say to each of them, "Do you know
what you are? You are a marvel."*

-Pablo Casals

Years ago I was asked by the leader of my youngest
daughter's Girl Scout troop to act as chaperone for an
overnight camping trip to the woods of South Georgia. It
rained – a lot. The leader asked me if I would present a
devotional to the eight girls that Sunday night. This was a
task I looked forward to a whole lot less than you can
imagine.

As I lay on my cot in our cabin that night, listening to the
girls' chattering, I wondered what I could possibly say to a
group of ten-year old girls that would be inspirational. As I

tried to pull mind and soul together, I realized that, even though it might not be what the leader had in mind, I wanted to share my thoughts about each girl's uniqueness. At least my words would be congruent with my thoughts and feelings.

I began to think about these eight small individuals, each of whom was responding to our situation in a different way. Watching their characters and personalities emerge, I was utterly charmed. What marvels they were! They accepted the rain or they didn't. They complained or they coped. I got in touch with the fact that you can't treat a child as if "all the apples in a bushel are the same." Each is different, yet all are okay.

The time came the next day, and we gathered at the group meeting spot, and I was feeling inspired. After asking the girls to move their seats to form a circle, I shared with them my thoughts about each of them. I told each one how special she was, and that I, too, was a special person. The girls and the other leaders listened. I said, "We will learn together this year. Though I'm the appointed leader, you will also teach me." And they did. I taught them, they taught me and we all learned.

The act of reviewing and expressing my insights about those girls had a profound effect on me. I became more appreciative of every person and more inclined to value and love others. This awareness carried over a few years later when I became a full-time classroom teacher – of ten-year-old fourth graders.

My dictionary defines *uniqueness* as "being the only one; without a like or equal." I find this definition empowering. The word, coined in the 17th century, began to take on significance for me during that camping trip with the Girl Scouts. The next time I was awakened to its power was when I heard a speaker mention the chances of an egg and sperm uniting to form – me.

I'd been attending a national teacher conference in San Francisco and was tired and bored. Sitting there in the auditorium for a closing keynote speech, I was weary and trying not to listen. The microphone was turned up loud, and so was the speaker.

"There are trillions and trillions of eggs and sperms in the world." Big deal, I thought, I know that. "Billions and billions of them never make it." Yeah, yeah. What else is new? "Just think: one of those eggs and one of those sperms got together – and made you!"

I sat up. Without hearing another word the speaker said, I began to ponder the fact that *I'd made it*. I thought: *If I'm unique, one of a kind, there must be some special work I have to do.* The next thought, equally simple, equally profound, was that each child in my classroom had made it too and therefore had a special mission in life to accomplish. These realizations had an enormous impact on me. They helped me to value myself and my students more, to love them more. It wasn't until I started teaching and observing children up close that I began to appreciate the magnitude of their differences. At times I found these differences almost overwhelming.

ANDREW'S STORY

I am a Teacher. I was born the first moment
that a question leaped from the mouth of a
child.
    . . . I am a paradox. I speak loudest when I
        listen the most. My greatest gifts are in
        what I am willing to appreciatively receive
        from my students.
    . . . And so I have a past that is rich in
        memories. I have a present that is
        challenging, adventurous and fun because
        I am allowed to spend my days with the
        future.
I am a teacher ... and I thank God for it every
day.

                           -- John W. Schlatter

"Andrew's leaving!" The children were calling out,
but I wasn't concerned. It was just another time that
Andrew had gotten frustrated over trying to do writing or
other "seat work" and had walked out of the glass doors at
the end of the room. I knew he would be back soon. I knew

he wasn't going to get into trouble and he never disappointed me.

It was 1972 and I was teaching in an open-space school in a classroom without walls. Those were the days before all the talk of Attention Deficit Disorder and other learning disabilities. Andrew would undoubtedly be labeled with ADD today and be a candidate for Ritalin or some other drug with side effects. I'd had children with problems in my classes, but none like his—an almost total inability to sit still. Other teachers tried to get Andrew to sit quietly in his seat, with no success. Somehow I knew from the start that he really could not do it, and that was okay with me. Sometimes I would just look over at him at his corner desk and smile.

There was something I knew about Andrew that I've never forgotten over all these years. I wonder, how did I know it then? I had a lot of love for Andrew. I don't know why, but he captured my heart early on. Perhaps I was attracted to him because he was not attentive to me. I didn't communicate that trustfulness verbally to him; rather it was a kind of "knowing" with me. I understood this child, and I knew that as soon as he got himself settled, he would return and do some of his work—not all of it, but some.

About four years ago my daughter ran into Andrew, and he asked her, "Are you Mrs. Toothman's daughter?" When she assented, he said, "Oh, she was a wonderful teacher." Of course that was music to my ears, but not just because it inflated my importance. Rather, it told me that the year we had together was good for Andrew.

Why did we get along so well? Was it just that I was able to cope with his inability to function in the "normal" classroom? It was very important to him to connect with me, to have someone close by who really loved him. We all need that. I allowed him to participate in the school environment in a way that respected what he needed. To this day I don't know how I knew that, nor do I know how he knew that. It was just the way it was. If you're able to love a child, you help him or her.

As I've said, some of us come into the world with a stamp on us that says, "You can teach all kinds of kids." I am grateful to have had Andrew as a student because he reinforced in me that notion.

As I write this I'm remembering two little girls who had a great need to appear at my desk at the beginning of each school day. It mattered not to them that I had things to do; they were driven by their need to be heard. (All children have this need, but these two had a greater need than most.) They wanted to tell me what they had for dinner, what Daddy said, what Mama did. They had one-of-a- kind, special circumstances and conditions of their lives which they wanted to get across to me.

As I look back I wonder, did I really pay attention to them, or did I just shoo them away in order to start my teaching? I probably did the latter; but if I had it to do over, I would pay more attention to their uniqueness just as I did with Andrew.

No doubt many people would not think twice about the notion that each person is unique, yet that one idea, simple yet profound, never ceases to fascinate me. I am convinced that this awareness can be transforming.

I AM SOMEBODY

I am somebody
I might be winning
I might be losing
Sometimes moving, sometimes cruising
But still I am somebody.
I might be young
I might be old
Sometimes shy
And sometimes bold
But still I am somebody.
I might be short
I might be tall
It might be summer
It might be fall
But still I am somebody.
I might be black
I might be white
I might be uptight
Sometimes wrong
And sometimes right
But still I am somebody.
I might be black
I might be brown
Sometimes up
And sometimes down
But still I am somebody.
It's not what I ought to be
I'm not what I'm gonna be
It's not what I hope to be
But thank God
It's not what I used to be.

FACE MY FACE

The art of pleasing requires only the desire.

-- Lord Chesterfield

I'm a believer in the power of attention. I believe that giving attention is one of the most helpful things we can do for others. Attention is more than seeing; it's focusing, concentrating on another person and being with him or her without judgment or evaluation.

Having someone focus completely on you can literally change your life in a very dramatic way. Capturing another human being's complete focus leads one to believe, "I am somebody and I am worthy." Whenever someone has done that for me in my life, it has changed me profoundly, and I have never forgotten it.

My early memories of getting full attention began with my father's recognition of things I did well. He was a very quiet man and often sat and observed without speaking. I recall when I would cook a meal for our family, he would look around, focus on me and comment softly, "Well, I know who cooked today."

I relearned the power of attention when I was talking about how to be a more effective parent to a group of parents. A young mother approached me to tell me that she wanted to attend any future parenting workshops I conducted. "When you were talking to us about the need to give our children attention," she said, "I remembered something that happened this morning as I was driving my children to school. My middle daughter was attempting to tell me something. Realizing I was distracted, she turned my face around with her little hands and said, 'Mother, face my face.'"

I was so moved by this mother's story, I asked her for permission to use it in my talks and writings. "Face my face" reminded me of Thornton Wilder's play, <u>Our Town</u>, when the girl who has died finds herself still at home observing her family's life without her. She keeps saying, "Mother, look at me." At the time, the face-my-face story added to my constantly growing conviction about the importance of attention in relationships with those we love and teach.

A few years ago I was conducting a class of teachers in communication skills and we were working on the concept of paying attention. One of the participants told this story:

When I was growing up, my little six-year-old brother Jimmy was just starting school, and he was quite thrilled about it. He even showed up the first day of school with a plant for his teacher.

But after a few weeks his teacher sent one of those "letters of doom" home to my parents. "Jimmy is not learning to read," the note revealed. "Please come to the school for a conference." When Mother showed up, the teacher told her that Jimmy would not pay attention in class.

That evening Mother sat down with Jimmy and told him what the teacher had said. My brother's response was, "She pays 'none' attention to me, so I pays 'none' attention to her." When school was over that year, Jimmy retrieved his plant and took it home with him.

We all enjoyed hearing the story of Jimmy, but the best was yet to come. His sister reported that once he got out of that classroom he did learn to read and was very successful in school. In fact, he became a nuclear physicist!

HERE CAME JOHN

The few teachers who meant the most to me in my school life were not necessarily those who knew the most, but those who gave out of the fullness of themselves; who confronted me face to face as it were, with a humanhood that awoke and lured my own small and trembling soul and called me to take hold of my existence with my two hands.

--Sydney J. Harris

One year I had a classroom running over with fourth graders and a principal who insisted that everything in the school be kept in apple-pie order. All school property was absolutely sacred. No talking in the hallways, silent lunches, teachers forbidden to walk down the hall with a cup of coffee—these were just some of the many rules. Into this strained situation came John, the child of seasonal workers who followed the fruit and vegetable picking throughout Florida.

My first glimpse of John was his face at the back of a long line of silent students who were lined up military style. John had not come from that culture and experienced difficulty in being "lined up." He had a great need to be at the front of that line and be one of the first to hug the teacher. In his effort to get to the front he would often knock books and lunch boxes out of the arms of fellow students. My heart reached him long before he got to me—but what to do? I was tuned in to his great need for love and attention, but how could I contain him without doing any damage? John seemed to be totally unaware of the impact his behavior had on the other students.

I was enrolled in a graduate course at the University of South Florida, working on a Master's degree, and in one of my courses I learned about behavior modification— the strategy of ignoring undesirable behavior while systematically rewarding the desired behavior . I developed a plan: don't speak to or acknowledge John unless he is walking silently in that straight line and sitting in his seat.

Then I would respond nonverbally--immediately move to him, look into his face, give him a hug, etc.

This seemed to work for a while. One day the principal came to my room to deliver a phone message. Unfortunately John was having difficulty getting to his seat through the crowded aisles and had chosen that moment to get there in a much quicker way—by stepping from the top of one desk to another. The principal was standing with me outside the classroom door. When she observed John's behavior, her immediate reaction was to "go for him." I literally held her back and said, "Please don't speak to John when he is behaving this way." I then explained to her the strategy I was using. As usual, she was fascinated by ideas that were forthcoming from "The University" and stayed a while longer to observe the outcome.

The behavior modification project did improve John's behavior, but he moved soon to the next work site with his parents so I was unable to form any long-term conclusions.

What told me to leave John to his own devices? I suppose one important ingredient was the respect I felt for him -- the respect I feel for all children. Each child is utterly unique. While he or she does need guidance and must learn to respect limits, that person must never be violated. All must be respected in every way. Only thus does the child come to respect himself or herself.

By patiently observing John's behaviors, I could eventually employ appropriate strategies for effectively dealing with his emotional needs.

I'm convinced that most teachers have this ability, but many react to the surface appearance or behavior of a child before they have a chance to truly observe him. It requires a certain level of self-control to stand back calmly and observe. Observing in this way doesn't mean being quiet, or passive. It often happens while you are busy talking, moving about the classroom and giving directions. My advice to teachers is: open yourself. Learn to observe each and every child. Look for the uniqueness in each. Trust yourself to respond with this awareness to the needs of each precious individual.

TEDDIE'S BROTHER

When we have done our best, we should wait the result in peace.

---J. Lubbock

Teddie was in my class one year and I had his younger brother the next. What was interesting was that while I felt successful with Teddie, when his brother came along I could tell that he was very different from Teddie and would be more difficult for me to reach and teach.

He was very independent (that's good, not bad) and he loved to draw. Drawing was how he really wanted to spend his time. One day he drew a picture of me on a bridge, and the caption under the picture said, "Keep walking off the bridge." He hoped I would get it, and I did. His meaning was that I should keep walking to my death!

This really disturbed me. I knew the family. The father was a doctor. I thought it over for a couple of days before I did anything. Then I discussed the situation with my principal--the same one who believed that silence was golden and that we would all be successful if we just obeyed the rules. She was distraught that this had happened and immediately called the parents. I felt a little funny about her doing that as they were close neighbors and we knew them well. My internal response was, "This is really going to be a mess!" Yet my rational side was telling me that this should be reported.

When the parents came to the school, the principal invited me to sit in on the conference. I was surprised when they immediately thanked me for bringing this incident to their attention. It turned out that they, too, had been getting similar messages from their child, as had other family members.

At this time, Teddie's brother would have been nine or ten years old. This situation really disturbed me. It wasn't fear that prompted my action. My thought process was that if one of my own children had done something like that, I would certainly want to know about it. I have since heard that this young man has become a professional cartoonist and is doing very well. I'm hopeful that this might have come about because his parents became actively involved in what was happening.

Of course I didn't know then about Columbine or other incidents of violence that would occur later in schools. In today's world, the warning I received would be considered a very scary message for a teacher and would be reported as a matter of policy. As teachers, we shouldn't be spending our time looking for this sort of behavior and putting labels on children. At the same time, we need to be acutely aware of possibilities.

Providing real attention is one of the gifts we can give. This attention says to the other person, " You are somebody, you are really worth something and what you have to say is valuable." How many children could be saved if one teacher took the time to pay "real" attention? However, when destruction of self or others is the child's message, supports need to be provided to get the help needed.

BILL THE INCORRIGIBLE

The thing always happens that you really believe in;
and the belief in a thing makes it happen.

-- Frank Lloyd Wright

When ten-year-old Bill arrived in my fourth-grade language arts class, his records showed a steady stream of behavior problems. The blue records showed that he had been thrown off every school bus he'd ever ridden. Typical of teachers' comments was, "Bill can't be trusted, led or taught." I wondered about this; Bill was a model of bright attention and favorable behavior while in my presence during language arts classes.

We were housed in an open-spaced school, so no one had any secrets. Bill sat in an imaginary corner of my room without walls, a few feet away from the library (from which, it was well known, Bill had long been banned). Whenever he was in physical education, I could see and hear all the ruckus he raised with the male phys. ed. teacher, who frequently banished Bill from his class. Another teacher delivered him almost daily to the principal's office to be paddled for misbehaving in her class.

One day a meeting was held at the school, attended by the district supervisors, a school psychologist and other authorities, to decide whether to transfer Bill to a special school designed to handle students who proved unmanageable in normal classroom situations. Overhearing the discussion, I decided to join the group.

"I never have trouble with Bill," I said to the others. "Please let me have him. I'll do an individual plan for his studies and be responsible for him in all areas of his learning." They looked at me in wonderment. "Bill will be fine with me," I smiled and assured them. The group agreed to give my plan a go.

By this time I knew quite a bit about this youngster's home situation. Bill's father was an alcoholic and his mother was borderline alcoholic. I knew that taking responsibility for his success in school was risky, but it proved to be one of the best things I ever did as an elementary school teacher.

As part of the agreement that he be assigned to my class, he was not to go to physical education with the other children or to another teacher for math. Bill was content with me as his "full-time" teacher and his school life stabilized. He was quiet and well behaved in my class. My expectations of Bill were positive; I did not expect him to behave in the ways his records reported. I never nagged him or reminded him of what he should be doing. I gave him an individualized program of work to do and he did it. Bill and I liked each other.

After some weeks had passed, Bill came to my desk and asked me if he could go to the library. Looking at my watch, I said, "Yes, but you'll need to be back in ten minutes." I then added, " And no trouble." Bill was back in the allotted time, and he had done fine. After that, he had permission to come and go alone to the library.

Everyone, myself included, was in awe as to how well he did in my classroom. My college-age son and his friend once came to my classroom to observe this miraculous transformation of Bill the Incorrigible to Bill the Model Student. My son still reminds me of how successful I was with Bill.

A few years later I ran into someone from the school where I worked. As we chatted he mentioned Bill. "I'll bet that kid is in prison," he said, shaking his head. "Well," I said, "he may be, but I don't think so. I'll bet he still remembers the one good year he had in my fourth grade class."

I've thought a lot about Bill, and I think I know the secret behind the phenomenal change in this student. Bill knew that I had rescued him when he was going to be sent to the alternative school. From the very start, he and I were communicating. He clearly knew my expectations for him, and that I accepted him totally. He had no privileges when he came to me. I gave him back some of the privileges he wanted, such as going to the bathroom and traveling the halls without accompaniment.

Part of the reason I had so much empathy for children like Bill was that I was a little like them as a student myself. I had been a prankster, letting air out of the school principal's tires and throwing snowballs down the aisle in high school. I even organized a day for many of the seniors to skip school, arranged a truck and got my sister's boy friend to drive us to Sulphur Springs. I wasn't perfect and I accepted others, like Bill, who weren't perfect either.

THE PERFECTIONIST

Of the good leader, the people will say,
"We did this ourselves."

-- *Confucius*

James, a tall fourth grader, was my only black student that year. A perfectionist, James was his own worst problem. He was painstaking about everything. For example, his math numerals had to be shaped perfectly and placed in precisely the right position. It was painful for me to watch his struggle to be so meticulous. James and I managed very well in my classroom, but he never wanted to go to physical education. Nothing in that class seemed "perfect" enough for James.

One day some students came running in from the playground to tell me that James was crying. I sensed right away that things out there had not been "lined up" to suit him, and he just couldn't cope. I went outside and positioned myself in front of all those upset children who were yelling, "James is crying again!" The bell rang, but I just stood there, my whole class gathered around me, until everyone was quiet. Then I asked, "Isn't it all right to cry? What if I were to cry some day, would that be all right?"

"Oh yes!" the children chorused. There and then we established a new norm; it's all right to cry when you feel like crying.

When we went inside, James proved he was not a quiet cryer. He put his head down on his desk and really let loose. Meanwhile, the rest of us went on with our work. After that, I don't recall another incident of James's crying. Still a perfectionist, he was less frustrated.

At least ten years after he was in my classroom, I received a phone call, on February 18th. A very refined and adult but unfamiliar male voice said, "Happy birthday, Mrs. Toothman!" I asked for the caller's identity; it turned out to be James.

"How did you know it was my birthday?" I asked.

"I have always known that," he replied.

I felt elated that one of my former students had called long-distance to wish me well. More than that, I was glad that my fourth graders and I had made crying and perfectionism acceptable behaviors. I learned from that episode with James that if you involve students in thinking about what is acceptable and unacceptable in the classroom, they will forever be with you in love and acceptance. Collaborating with students in rule-setting eliminates the need to enforce the rules. Because of this student involvement, my classroom became a comfortable place, for both me and the students.

VICTORIA

Treat me like I do--and I will.
Treat me like I don't--and I won't!

As I opened the classroom door on my first day of substitute teaching in a new school, I saw a beautiful girl with large black eyes and gorgeous black skin pulled taut over her cheekbones. Her black hair was twigged and clamped with pins of many colors. Behind her stood a line of 33 children of all descriptions.

"You are old," this young lady said to me the moment she saw me. "I don't like old people, and I don't like substitutes!"

The voices of those behind her chorused, "Victoria, you shouldn't say things like that to a teacher!"

"Well, Victoria," I said calmly, looking her in the eye. "I don't think you like me." My voice, I knew, conveyed that the greeting this young lady had given me was acceptable to me. I could sense she didn't quite know how to handle having the ball returned to her own court so swiftly after having delivered such an aggressive outburst.

The children came inside and the day's instruction began. We'd barely established some semblance of order when a small boy yelled out, holding up his thumb with the blood dripping from it. Victoria had chosen to vent her frustration by biting another student. With Victoria in tow, I headed for the principal's office.

Hearing the administrator say, "Well, Miss Victoria!" as we entered his office, I sensed I was witnessing a usual scene between these two, and that the approach of the administrators was only reinforcing this girl's sense that she was expected to be disruptive.

Victoria did not return to the room until late afternoon, accompanied by the male assistant principal. Her beautiful black face was swollen from crying. It seemed she had experienced another bout of trouble with the front office after kicking three children in the clinic. The man sternly insisted that she apologize to me. Something in me rose up in protest. I said, "Victoria, I want you to go and wash your face; and when you feel like it, we will talk." This she did.

As the end-of-the-day bell rang, Victoria emerged from the clinic. She came to me and said, "I would like to do something for you. My mama says that I'm really good at cleaning up." Fifteen minutes later all the books, puzzles and other debris were cleared away, and I was commending my young friend for her help.

Victoria walked up to me and said, "I think I like you."

I responded, "I think I like you, too."

She put her arms around my waist. "I really want to hug you," she said.

"I want to hug you, too, Victoria."

Victoria reminded me of a lesson that I had learned long ago. She was saying her truth when she encountered me as her substitute teacher. She did not like old people and she did not like substitute teachers. Her intention was not meant to demean me; she was honest as she communicated to me. Apologies that are forced on children are ineffective.

My disapproval of forcing her to apologize made Victoria want to do something for me. As I showed this child acceptance and caring we were able to work out our issues together. Victoria learned so much that day and so did I. I will be forever grateful to her.

I've told this story to groups of teachers. As they listened to the way Victoria greeted me that morning, some of them have reacted, "You let her speak to you that way?" Doubtless this little girl expected me to come down on her, as others had. My intuition told me she had made herself feared through such behavior. When I let her say what she thought without reprimanding her, it stopped the game. When I saw what happened later in the office, I was glad I hadn't fallen into the pattern of reaction. Sometimes the strength of a teacher's influence lies in letting children *be*.

DONNIE

The only way to help someone be what they want to be is to accept them as they are.

--Charlene Kilpatrick, Classroom Teacher

I can still see this child coming out of the bathroom near my classroom with his thick blonde hair hanging down over his eyes, looking as if he could hardly see. I recall my feeling, "Oh, Donnie, get that hair out of your eyes!" His whole appearance was repugnant to me.

Donnie was a shy little guy; he looked like someone had literally beaten the life out of him. I had a hunch that he'd been abused, but I didn't pay attention to my intuition until it was almost too late.

What finally woke me up happened on the day I sent a note home to his mother: "Donnie needs to do better." When he came to class the next day, he was bruised all over. His little legs bore welts from having been strapped with a belt. He merely said to me in his quiet way, "Mrs. Toothman, I hope you will send a good note home with me today." I could hardly hold the tears back as I said, "You can bet your life on it, Donnie." And I did.

In the days that followed I began to do things to change my attitude toward this child. Sometimes we really have to study children – all people, in fact – in order to let the good things about them be there for us. We are all unique, and we come into the world with a special stamp on us. I asked myself, "What is Donnie's special design in his life? What is it about this boy that makes him special?"

In time, I no longer noticed the hair in his eyes or the fact that he wasn't quite as bright as some of his classmates. Those weren't the things I was looking for. Instead, I began looking to discover all the things he was doing right – and you know, there were a lot of them!

What really happened, once I started to change, was that I started loving Donnie. I started appreciating his silence, his sense of solitude, his bravery in the face of what he'd been dealt. He also began contributing in class when I changed my attitude toward him. Also, I began to be grateful for the life lesson he was teaching me. Before the end of the year, Donnie and I were friends. I had accepted him as a unique child that I loved.

I've often wondered since then, "What might have happened if I hadn't awakened? What if I'd continued to send those 'bad notes' home? What if I hadn't been able to observe the consequences? What would have happened to Donnie? What would have happened to me?"

Throughout my life I have been given gifts of acceptance by others. Because I grew up feeling that I was loved and that I was okay, I was able to convey that acceptance strongly to others. As a teacher, I was able to give that gift to students. I was able to accept children as they were, without needing to remodel or fix them.

When I could offer children my total acceptance, they were able to grow and develop and learn. Also, I did not struggle with behavior problems from them. Without acceptance, children are blocked. True acceptance means looking beyond the obvious and seeing the wonderful, one-of-a-kind person that is there. We need to find adults who can work with children like Bill and Victoria by showing them sincere respect and caring.

JONAH, THE SURVIVOR

If you can dream it, you can do it.

-- Walt Disney

I was a first-year teacher and busy with getting to know the school and my work. It was right after President Kennedy was assassinated that the father of one of my fourth grade students, in the presence of his whole family, put a gun to his head and shot himself. His son, Jonah, was bright, precocious, good looking and creative. I did not have a close relationship with him, but after the incident I made a real effort to build a bond with him. I saw great potential in Jonah.

I never saw Jonah cry; I wondered how such a sensitive child would cope with his tragedy. He showed great bravery as he returned to school, but he stayed close to me. He began devoting much time to his writing; I wondered what it was about. Finally Jonah showed his work to me. As he did so, he said with perfect confidence, "Some day when I run for election as President of the United States I'll deliver this speech."

When I read Jonah's speech, I realized that he had connected his own pain with that of the Kennedys and a stunned nation. Despite his own pain, his words rang with conviction.

Following is Jonah's speech, just as he wrote it:

INOGRAL ADDRESS

People of the United States. I thank you for electing me president of the United States. I accept. I accept to become the 35th president of the United States. I promise you good leadership and be your good friend. I will try to stop pollution. I will beat Russians to Mars. I will try to do everything possible that is good for this country. I would like you to help me. I quote what John F. Kennedy once said Ask not what your country can do for you. Ask what you can do for your country. Thank you. I understand that right now Moscow is in a *continuous war with the United States. I will try,*

as the President of the United States should to make

friends with Moscow. Dropping the subject of

Moscow, I conclude that I will understand that the

Russians are at a endless fight to have the first one

to Mars. I intend to win that fight. And if you do

not believe in what I am saying you can say "well,

who cars who wins." I care. And that proves that

you do not respect this Nations Heritag. And also

do not believe in the flag. Why in the world do you

think they made the pledge of alligennce to the flag.

So you would have something to say "I love this

nation" to. I will stop wars. I ask for your help. If

mankind does not stop war, war will stop mankind.

If we try we can escape this.

I continued to love Jonah and remained close to him
and his mother for several years. Today as I write this I
wonder where he is and how he is faring. I'm sure that
somewhere he is still using that tremendous strength and

courage he demonstrated when he was in my fourth grade. He is out there somewhere doing more than just coping.

I was in awe of how Jonah took care of himself. My role was to be with him. I had no advice ("Don't be sad," etc.). He found out on his own what he needed to do to heal his wounds. We all have had pain and learned that it does not help to have people advise us to get over it. So many of the instructions teachers have for children are so ineffective. We need to recognize the knowledge that is already inside children. Often if we do less for them, we find out what they can do for themselves.

SNITZKERS

Let me not neglect any kindness,
For I shall not pass this way again.

George Elliott

It was just before Christmas, and my fourth grade children made ready to leave for the holidays. One by one they came up to my desk to leave their little gifts and cards and love notes. Most were glowing with smiles and comments. One student, Thelma, shyly left her card without a smile or spoken word. I smiled, thinking, *"How typical of her."*

A few days later, as I was doing my Christmas baking, my husband Rex was reading through the cards. He said to me, "Here's a funny one from Thelma. It says, 'Thank you for all the snitzkers you have given us.'" Rex and I looked at each other in puzzlement. Neither of us had any idea what "snitzkers" were. He suggested that I ask Thelma what she meant when school began again.

On the first day back from the holidays, I chose a moment when the other students were busy to approach Thelma. I thanked her for the card and asked, "What are snitzkers?"

She motioned for me to bend down; then she whispered in my ear, "Love and kindness."

The children and I had been discussing the origin of words, and I had told them that before the airplane was invented there had been no name for it. Being sensitive to Thelma's shy, quiet nature, I whispered back to her, "I would like for you to write your word on the board." She got right up and did so. As her classmates stared, I publicly complimented Thelma on creating a new word. She seemed very pleased.

Snitzkers soon became a word used daily by the whole class. As I met the class lined up outside my classroom door each morning, they would interpret my mood. If they thought it was positive, they would say, "We're gonna get lots of snitzkers today!" I would wrinkle my nose in approval. When they sensed a more negative mood, they'd say, "We won't get many snitzkers today."

It's possible that Thelma's word for love and kindness was from another language or dialect spoken in her home. That didn't matter to me. What mattered was the recognition she received. It proved to have a magical effect on her shyness and lack of confidence. That precious little girl and the word she brought us turned out to be a blessing on my classroom that year.

As the teacher, I was in the background, providing the love and kindness so that this miserably shy little girl felt safe enough to send me her original word. By my asking her in a quiet way to share the word and its meaning to her with the class, her light started to shine. The students looked to her then as a person with intelligence and talent. If teachers are alert, they can help students become stars.

Every person needs a mission —an overarching statement of purpose that touches every area of life. My mission is to continue to make a difference in the lives of children, one that can only be accomplished by those who

care deeply about them and their needs and circumstances.

SPECIAL-ED SUBSTITUTE

How do you reach them? The troubled ones –
The hurt ones –The lonely ones –The beaten ones –
How do you reach them?
You listen with your heart. You share their burden.
You change their screams to dreams –
Dreams, and promise, and hope!

Dedicated to Nelda Toothman who gave us the skills to reach them.

-- Barbara Governale

"Nelda, could you come in tomorrow and teach our special education class? Miss Spencer is sick." My answering machine gave me this message one evening when I returned home. I thought about it. I had never taught a special ed class but decided to give it a go.

Arriving at the school, I was delighted to recognize the two paraprofessionals who would assist me. Both had been participants in a special training program I had designed and facilitated the previous summer. As they were knowledgeable about the classroom and students we would teach, I felt very secure as we started off. Though my heart hurt a lot that day, I learned much.

The class exhibited a wide variety of exceptional situations, both mental and physical. One student, a handsome young man named Ralph, was about the age of a fifth-grader. He had a storehouse of rage and bitterness I'd never before encountered in a child. As I sat outside with him on the classroom steps, my attention totally focused on him, the "active listening" skills I had taught in many Teacher Effectiveness Training programs stood me in good stead.

"I hate this place," he muttered. "I hate my regular teacher. I hate my parents, too." As his hate list unfolded, I could not help feeling that he belonged under the care of a psychotherapist. Then he paused and added, "I'd rather have you."

Several times during the day a huge boy named Larry would pass me and pat my shoulder lovingly, like a small child. Opposite in size to this gentle giant was a precious

Downs Syndrome child named Gerald, who reminded me of a neighbor boy when I was growing up who'd been similarly handicapped. I'd always admired that boy's family because of their deep affection for him; they took him everywhere they went, utterly unashamed of his appearance and erratic behavior.

Gerald approached me early in the day and gestured, "Come here." Motioning to a pair of stools by a table he said, "Sit down." I sat. Shoving a pack of oversized cards toward me, Gerald said, "Deal cards." I reached for the pack, but he quickly smiled and said, "I deal!" As he went through the motions, I smiled, tickled to be invited into his little program.

While my card-sharp friend dealt himself a pile of cards, he gave me only three. This disparity, and the fact that I was never permitted to look at the faces of my cards, was apparently part of the rules. Watching, I learned that the game consisted of taking turns flicking cards down on the table. What was important to my new friend was that he was in charge of things.

In a few minutes he announced, "I win!" I offered to deal the next hand, just to see his reaction. Not surprisingly he replied, "No. I deal." As he proceeded to chalk up more wins, Gerald laughed out loud often. Each time he chuckled, I had to resist the impulse to gather him up in my arms.

Gerald interrupted his game-playing several times to show concern about a classmate, another Downs Syndrome student named Elise. When I arrived that morning I had noticed her feet sticking out from under the teacher's desk. Special education teachers don't sit at their desks as a rule, so I waited. After an hour or two I asked the aide about Elise. We were finally able to move the desk and get her out. What impressed me was Gerald's reaction. He got up, crossed the room and put his little arms around Elise. He hugged and hugged her until she bent low enough for him to kiss her.

Tears sprang to my eyes, for I recognized that these two children had something very special between them, a gentle and understanding love which I believe is often displayed by Downs Syndrome children.

Never again would I be reluctant or fearful about working with special needs students. They teach us about ourselves. Being around them is being in the presence of truth.

CONFRONTING UNACCEPTABLE BEHAVIOR

Accept the challenges so that you may feel
the exhilaration of victory.

--General George S. Patton

Several years ago I was teaching an adult class of educators. As we were studying listening skills and communication, the classroom activities engaged the participants in working with partners or small groups to practice the skills. By the second day of the class, I found my enthusiasm was being depleted by the actions of an older man who had told us he was taking the class to earn credit towards substitute teaching.

Each time I asked the members of the class to engage in an activity, this fellow would sigh loudly and pick up his briefcase to move, looking bored at the thought of being asked to be actively engaged in learning. Observing my own reaction, I found I was losing my energy for teaching the class. That night as I ate my dinner alone I thought about what I had to do.

In the morning, again observing the man's behavior, I moved close to him so that I could talk to him quietly one-on-one. I said, "I have been hired to teach this class and the activities included are designed for your learning. I've noticed that every time I announce an activity, you breathe a big heavy sigh, pick up your briefcase and move slowly to work with the others, looking as though you will die of boredom. Your behavior affects me in a very negative way. I find I can't quite be myself when you react that way. I would appreciate your cooperation."

Following my confrontation, he stopped the behavior. The class went on, my energy came back and I felt like my normal self. When the class ended, I discovered I had failed to pass out certificates to the teachers. The teachers were heading out the door, but this gentleman quickly offered to call them back. He went to the stairway and yelled loudly; then, returning to the classroom, he said to me, "You sign the certificates and I will pass them out." He did so, and we became friends.

Later that night I read the journals of the participants in the class and several commented on my interaction with the student. Weeks later several of the teachers commented on what they had learned from my confronting the offending participant. These teachers reported that from my modeling they learned they could do the same with their students.

A second instance will help to make this point. Once when I was teaching a Leader Effectiveness Training (LET) class to school administrators, I had a man in the class who was something of a glad-hander. From the opening, he would sit in the back of the room against the door with one long leg out in the aisle and start telling jokes. He was one of those we call in the South a good ol' boy. This behavior put me off, so I approached him and said, "When you sit in the back, you always seem to be making conversation, and this is distracting for me and for the rest of the class. I would appreciate it very much if you moved up toward the front and took more of a part in what we are doing." Not only did the participant comply immediately, the next day he brought me a big bouquet of roses! My soft yet firm approach had worked.

Confrontation is a marvelous skill for teachers to develop, to displace the "making wrong" associated with teacher reprimanding. It can be adapted for any student's age or background and done in a gentle way. If someone's behavior is a drain on your energy, that person needs to know how they are affecting you. The best approach is a combination of tough and nice. Don't say too much or try to soften the blow. Be firm and at the same time respectful. Describe the specific behavior that is unacceptable and tell how it is affecting you. The objective of the confrontation should be to help the students know how their behavior affects your teaching.

PEER LEARNING

People do not want to be managed;
they want to be led.

--UTC message in *Wall Street Journal*

Her name was Mary Johnson, and she was a sure-fire teacher. The only black teacher in an all-white school, Mary was color-blind, exuding respect and love for each of her students. The impression she made was of someone who was neither black nor white. I loved her for that; it was unusual, in the South in those days. She was simply a great person, a true professional, a teacher of the very finest order.

I've had such deep relationships with black people throughout my life that sometimes I wonder if I'm black myself. There was Weeden, of course, when I was little. Another—one I could write another book about—was Cora, a woman who worked for me for years when my children were little. Cora was as cross as two sticks. She never smiled, and always treated me with a sort of impatience.

She used to tell me things like, "If you don't know how to wash, I can't iron for you!" Cora embodied that matriarchal attitude many Southern black women had in those days. I always felt the deep friendship for me that was behind her orneriness.

But Mary, as I say, was different. She and I had open-space classrooms that were barely separated by files and partial walls. I was a relatively new teacher then, and Mary became my example for many techniques I've used ever since. One was her constant 'positivity.' She was always full of joy and she showed it. I used to listen to her voice and think, "How can she be so happy this morning?" I may have been feeling down – and showing it – but Mary always seemed to be up when and if children were involved. They would come to school each day with their arms outstretched to hug her. She loved those children, and they knew it.

Mary also really cared about the other teachers. She modeled cooperation for all of us. She was a delight. Wherever you are, Mary, my hat's off to you. Your life was evidence to me that love is the same no matter the color of the students or the teacher. If you ever should read this, perhaps you'll understand that you made a difference in my life. You taught me things I never learned from anyone else. You didn't intend to – but I learned anyway.

THE POWER OF AFFIRMATION: ZINK & SISTER JOSETTA

A word spoken in due season,
How good it is.

-- Proverbs 15:23

I was sitting in my office where I worked as a supervisor of the school volunteer program, when a group of secretaries came running down the hall and said excitedly, "Nelda, come quick. There's a man giving a speech down in the civic center, and he's talking just like you do!" When I arrived, the speaker was telling a story about himself and I sat down to listen to it.

"I was in the fifth grade at Our Lady of Grace elementary school," he said, "and Sister Josetta was my teacher. Every day we would wait, standing by our desks, until Sister would enter the room at the back and come forward very quietly. Then we would sit down.

'Good morning, children,' Sister would say, scooting her feet softly as she moved to the center of the room. We all watched, fascinated, as she held up her ten fingers and said, 'Today we are going to work on ten projects. I've listed them on the board. Please copy them down now.' We all went to work and copied the list. Then Sister Josetta would say, 'When you finish the first project, I want you to take your colored pencil and draw a line through it on your list.' We all did as Sister said, working carefully along and checking off each item. Near the end of the list always came the 'dessert' – a favorite long-term project we were working on."

The speaker paused as if remembering. Then he smiled and went on. "There was one thing Sister did that I never forgot. One day she came over to me and stood admiring the work I'd done. She put her hand on my shoulder, looked into my eyes and said, 'Zink, I think you are going places.'" The man's voice trembled as he said this, and he actually wiped his eyes.

"And you know," he finally continued, "I *have* gone places. I've traveled all over the world. I've written seven books, and I want to tell you something. As teachers, we never know how one affirming thing we say can alter a student's life."

I doubt that most teachers or parents realize the power they have to influence how children see themselves and what they think is possible. Of course we're never fully aware at the time of how a certain interaction with a student may result in a "moment of truth" for him or her. If we could just stay awake, though, to the fact that it's possible, perhaps we would try to create more positive turning points than negative ones.

STUDENT FEEDBACK

Feedback is the breakfast of champions.

– Ken Blanchard

I often run into young adults who were once my students. Recently, Beth, a teacher in a nearby school, sent word to me that her experiences as a child in my fourth grade classroom were the cause of her becoming a teacher.

Not long ago I was in a Chinese restaurant and encountered the chef, a former student named Tommy. I remembered that he was a free spirit as a fourth grader and I always believed life would be good to him. He leaned across the counter, wrapped his long octopus-like arms around me and said, "You haven't changed a bit." (A real diplomat that Tommy.) Then he added, "I've just returned from studying some career choices in France. You opened up the world for me by sharing your own travels with us back then." And it was the truth; I had told all about our travels to my class. I showed pictures of Europe and talked about incidents we experienced or people we met.

My husband Rex and I were attending a wedding reception when a young man in his twenties approached me. It was John, a former fourth grade student of mine. He beamed and said, "Do you know what I remember about you, Mrs. Toothman?"

"I'm almost afraid to hear it," I joked.

"Oh no," he reassured me, "I remember that you liked me." As I reflected on what he had said, I thought I must have. I also thought it was a gift that every teacher could give every child.

Another former student, Eddie, told me that he never forgot the time he failed to bring his homework to my class and was anxious about it. "You told me it was okay," he said grinning. "You said you didn't remember my missing an assignment before that."

Teachers usually don't get to see or hear about the impact that their work has made on their students, but I have been very fortunate in that respect. These examples of affirmation all came to me twelve or more years after my time with these students. I don't need to tell you that each one gladdened my heart. I am sad that often when students grow up and sing their praises, many teachers are not around to hear the music. As I continue looking back in wonder from this stage of life, I want to pause and muse upon the power of affirmations. Perhaps you have been as fortunate as I have, to be a receiver of one of these potent gifts.

An affirmation is a statement given to someone which proves that he or she is one of a kind. The power of an affirmation lies in its ability to help shape the way we see ourselves. Affirmations tell us we are created to do certain kinds of positive things in the world. They are not merely compliments; they are validations of the truth of what we are.

One strong affirmation came my way when I was in my sixties. I was conducting a class on Long Island with a large group of teachers. Just before lunchtime the group gave me a standing ovation. At the break a young Indian man followed me up the stairs, took my elbow and said, "Nelda, any time you can move sixty tired Long Island teachers to their feet, you need to pay attention to what you've got!" I've never forgotten that affirmation; it made me reflect on my ability to work with large audiences. I still have intentions of doing more of that in my years ahead.

Parents have a unique opportunity to observe what is special about a child and comment on it. Looking back on my interactions with my own children, I wish I had been better at identifying and affirming each one's unique characteristics and gifts.

A hundred years from now it will not matter what my bank account was, the sort of house I lived in, or the kind of car I drove. But the world may be different because I was important in the life of a child.

-- Anonymous

STORIES ABOUT NELDA

"Who are you?" said the caterpillar. Alice replied rather shyly,
"I-I hardly know sir, just at present – at least I know who I was
when I got up this morning, but I must have
changed several times since then."

--Lewis Carroll

To love what you do and feel that it matters—
how could anything be more fun?

--Katherine Graham

Every piece of serious writing is in a sense autobiographical,
in that it has to be derived from the intuition and experience
of the person who wrote it…It is something that your own
experience of life compels you to write."

--Tennessee Williams

At this point in my life I am looking back on my really joyous years of teaching and wondering why I was the kind of teacher who created an atmosphere for students that created the stories in this book. I am an 80-year-old lady who finds herself wondering why she was the kind of teacher she was – the kind who did not ever embarrass or humiliate her students, but who kept order, imparted knowledge, and earned the respect and love of students.

Hopefully these "about Nelda" stories will help others to understand how my life experiences have influenced my teaching career.

THE "LITTLE SEAMSTER"

Some information about my early life may shed light on how my teaching career developed. My birthplace was the tiny community of Goodnight, Kentucky. We used to say that Goodnight was "seven miles from Glasgow, seven miles from Hiseville, and seven miles from Cave City." It wasn't much more than a wide place in the road, consisting of Crenshaw's and Quigley's grocery stores and Bledsoe's filling station.

Our house, situated on a dairy farm, had only the bare necessities (it was a big day when we got electricity!), but it was comfortable. My father, using knowledge he'd gained from his agriculture course at Western State College, grew apricots, peaches, cherries, grapes and asparagus. We also raised geese and turkeys and incubated baby chicks in our basement.

Most people can name key formative experiences from their early years. What comes to mind that influenced my life later as a teacher is simply the word *love*. My childhood was no different from most youngsters of that era who were reared on farms. I cooked, milked cows and plucked feathers from Mama's geese to make pillows. (To this day I still sleep on one of these down pillows.) The many happy hours I spent playing house with my doll family were often interrupted when Mother's shrill voice called me to stop playing and bring in wood or water. But growing up, I never once doubted that I was okay.

I was a very tiny little girl, and my relatives treated me as something of a mascot. (When I was five my cousin William and his friend James, eighth-graders at the time, used to put me in a chair and carry me in and out of the school building.) I learned early on that I could please people by performing; my two uncles gave me coins for showing off my ability to Charleston.

My saintly grandmother spent considerable time in our home, and I looked to her as my example. She and my kindly but taciturn father were the models I drew upon later when I began my teaching. Both provided guidance by their gentleness and absence of controlling.

At least three families lived in tenant houses on our farm, the male members working on the land for us. Of all the workers who moved through those years, I mostly remember Weeden who was Black, Charlie and Zulie who were White, and the Coomer family whom I grew to love.

I used to give Mrs. Coomer's two daughters shampoos and permanents and often made clothes for them. No one else in my family sewed, and I figured everything out on my own. I did my sewing on a pedal machine, learning by myself without instruction. When I was nine I made my first dress; it was red with black buttons. Mrs. Coomer used to say, "Nelda is the most wonderful little seamster!"

Though I got a kick out of her pronunciation of the word seamstress, her calling attention that way meant a lot to me. That original word "seamster" seemed to stand for my initiative, my willingness to figure things out on my own and do them with a will. I would think of it when, during several periods of my life, I created income for myself in a

variety of ways.   The "little seamster" has never been idle!

AFFIRMING WORDS

Throughout the early grades I attended a one-room school, and I was never any great shakes as a student. Nevertheless, it was assumed that my sister and I would attend college. To qualify for high school we had to take a county examination at the end of eighth grade. I was very scared, but I did well. (I always wondered if my father's being one of the school trustees had something to do with that.) After graduating from Hiseville High in the spring of 1939, I registered as a freshman at Western Kentucky State Teachers College (now Western Kentucky University).

My lack of study skills caught up with me very early in my college career. "Miss Church, will you please see me after class?" I can still feel the fearfulness of hearing my professors say that. After one semester I was hanging by a thread. History was the only class I actually failed, but when my mother received my grades in the mail she phoned and said, "Come home. You're only wasting money."

I'm a believer in the power of attention. We don't really see most people, nor are we truly seen by most. That's why, when someone completely focuses on you and speaks from that attention, you remember their words the rest of your life. I discovered this the day after my mother told me to give up college. As I was packing to leave, I heard my landlady greet my father and invite him in. "Please don't take Nelda home," she whispered.

My father and I sat down on the couch in the living room. "I've been looking at your grades, honey," he said, "and I don't think they're so bad."

"You don't?" I said.

We sat there for a minute or so, my father being a man of few words. Finally he said, "Did I ever tell you about the time I left college and took a job selling popcorn and peanuts on a train?"

I assured him that he had not. We sat for another while. At last he looked at me and said, "Well, you are bright, and I don't want you to come home." Reaching into his hip pocket, he pulled out a new checkbook and handed it to me. "The money's in the bank," he said. "It's yours."

Parents have the power to influence how children see themselves and what they think is possible. Teachers have it as well. The confidence my father showed in me became something to live up to. His brief words came back to me again and again as I worked hard the next semester and made some good grades. I'm sure my father's example of confidence and kindness shone down the years and touched my relationships with the children I taught.

WEEDEN

Growing up in the South, I was sensitive to the prejudice and oppression of Black people I saw going on around me. I often felt shame when members of my own family displayed these attitudes. One incident involved Weeden, a Black man who lived on our farm. Weeden could do the choo-choo dance. One Thanksgiving my sister brought some of her friends home from college. She called Weeden to come and dance in the snow for the visitors. When I saw him, I felt awful that we had imposed on him this way. He had no socks, and his bare toes were sticking out of his shoes. As I watched him dance, it was as if I could feel the cold in my own toes.

Mother gave him a hog jowl to pay for his dancing, and the matter was forgotten. But years later, whenever I recalled this incident with my sister, I felt shame. I think it heightened my sensitivity to others less fortunate than I.

DRY FORK SCHOOL

In the summers I took jobs in chain stores (like Newberry's and Woolworth's) in Glasgow, Kentucky. I sold shoes, worked as a bookkeeper and stocked hardware. My precious father drove me to all these jobs.

In 1942 the world was in an uproar; the conflict touched people's lives in countless ways. Some were tragic, others were formative. One day I received an urgent phone call from Max Ritter, the school superintendent. "Nelda," he said, "I want you to go immediately to teach at the school at Dry Fork. That damn teacher I had there has gone off to the war!" I decided immediately to place my college career temporarily on hold and take the job.

Dry Fork was a typical one-room school about twelve miles from Glasgow. Once again I called on my father, and we drove there on a rainy Sunday. As we slid about the muddy dirt roads, he started to grumble at me for the first time in my life. "Nelda, I don't want you to take this job.

Country people expect teachers to know everything!" He spoke from personal experience, for he'd been a country schoolteacher himself. "Your math is not good, and farmers will ask you to give them estimates on how much corn is in their cribs." He thought a moment and added, "Well, you *could* phone me and I could do the figuring for you."

As we approached the Dry Fork community my father said, "I'm going to stop at the first house I see that has electricity. That's where you'll stay." Sure enough, he did just that. The family's name was Morrison and they welcomed me with open arms. I had an attic room with a bed, dresser and small heater. I took my meals with the family. Willie D. was the oldest son, and then came George who was in high school.

I started my new job the next day. The school building was very much like the one I had attended in Goodnight. I didn't know much about what I should do as a teacher, but I was there to work and gradually, as I set my mind to it, the little seamster began to figure it out. It was a little like making that red dress with the black buttons. It was at this point in my life that I began using three basic principles: (1) act like you know; (2) be responsible; and (3) don't be afraid to make mistakes.

As I stood at the front of the class of bright faces that first day, I wasn't sure whether I was their fellow student – the same flighty school girl I used to be when I sat in a class like this – or their teacher. On the soft stream of that confusion, my heart flowed out to each of them in a natural love. I knew they felt it, too, for their gracious little hearts answered in incessant compliments.

Then little Lee Royce would arrive late. To induce a more pleasant look on my face, he would come right up to me and smile. Stroking my arm with his little dingy hands he'd say, "Miss Church, you wear the prettiest beads and pins." Among the pins that Lee Royce liked so much was a pair of gold wings like the ones that so many of our boys wore who flew the planes in World War II. Since December 7, 1941, all the proof any girl needed that she knew a nice young man was a symbol like my gold wings.

Teaching at Dry Fork was far more beneficial to me than any college courses could have been. Each day I walked the two and a half miles from the Morrisons' to the school, often wearing snow boots contributed by Mrs. Morrison. A young retarded student named Gillis built the fires for me each morning. He was a sort of assistant to me, very sweet and helpful.

The students ranged from a set of 5-year-old twins to 17-year-olds. I found right away that I loved those students, and they loved me. I recently received a letter from a woman who had been a young girl in that classroom. She still recalled the thrill of seeing new curtains being hung in the windows. I had taken my sewing machine along and used it to decorate.

WORKING AT KENRAD

After I left Dry Fork, the war years interrupted my college studies once again. I took a defense job at a newly opened KenRad plant in Bowling Green making radio tubes. The seamster's digital dexterity served me well in this tedious work. Within a few months I had learned all components of the assembly operation and was instructing the 66 women who worked my shift. I found this teaching easy and enjoyable, and my charges seemed to appreciate my patience as I worked with them.

From Dry Fork to KenRad was a tough adjustment. The stress of assembly-line procedures got to me, and I would often cry as my father drove me home from work. I've always been glad for that experience, however; it taught me that establishing positive relationships was critical to success, and that I was good at it.

Once again, my father had been a guiding light in my life. He had encouraged me to take the KenRad job. He often traveled to the counties where I recruited for the plant and talked to the people with whom I was involved. His constant affirmation, which I believed implicitly, was, "You know, honey, these people really love you."

MARRIAGE AND FAMILY

My husband Rex and I met while he was teaching at the Business University in Bowling Green. Rex had taken a teaching position at Florida Southern College in Lakeland during our engagement, so we began our married life in Florida. During that first summer I did some substitute teaching at a "strawberry school" near our home, so-called because the students who attended were the children of local farmers who grew strawberries. Their vacation time was scheduled in January and February so they could help with the picking.

Our life in Lakeland moved along, and within a few years we were the parents of three wonderful children. Later while living in Tallahassee, Florida, our family was also joined by a 17-year-old foster son, who had hitchhiked to Tallahassee from Costa Rica. In ensuing decades we have become the grandparents of four precious children.

Along the way there have been many smiles and also some tears. I consider myself a good wife, mother and grandmother, but I inwardly smile whenever I hear someone speak of a "perfect family." I know that there is no such thing. Imperfection is a part of life, and it is certain to be a part of a family. As I noted before, my own tolerance of imperfection has been a strength for me. Aware of my own faults, I never looked for others to be faultless.

GOD IS LOVE

A human life is like a storybook journey. Looking back, I recognize certain pivotal experiences that helped me to move on from a point where I was obstructed to the next chapter in the tale. One such event occurred in the late fifties while we were still living in Lakeland, when I enrolled in a course at Florida Southern entitled Religion in Modern Life.

My experiences with organized religion during my growing-up years had not endeared me to churchly ways. I believe in God, but I am repelled by those aspects of religion that separate people and result in bitterness, intolerance, even war and killing. Despite these misgivings, there in Lakeland I felt an urge to explore life's larger meaning for myself.

The instructor of the course, a Methodist preacher, impressed me little. The content of the course was interesting, but it was what happened after class that moved me. On three different occasions, as I was preparing to drive home from class, I got in the car, started it, then sat back and looked out the windshield. A clear impression would come to me, almost as if it were being spelled out in letters on the window, that GOD IS LOVE. I took this as a personal message: *You need not know what is ahead, but it is time to move on with your life.*

Shortly after I completed that course, we did move. Rex's new job with the Florida Department of Education took us to Tallahassee. There, in very uncharacteristic fashion, I became active in the Women's Society of the local Methodist church. Again something occurred which made me thankful I am impressionable and open to new learning.

As the South became embroiled in the issue of racial integration, I felt compelled to participate but didn't know just how. Indignant at the injustice and oppression of Black people, I wondered what, if any, role I was to play in helping resolve the problems. One evening after a church meeting on integration, I spoke to the minister about my feelings. That wonderful man smiled, held out his short arms and said, "Nelda, I can only help as far as these arms of mine can reach. If I tried to do more, they'd have to come and carry me off in a little white jacket."

That statement was something I was supposed to hear. It helped me to see that, while I need to take responsibility for what is truly within my power to change or improve, the world's problems are not in my hands. The serenity prayer came to me, "Give me the courage to change the things I can, the serenity to accept the things I cannot change, and the wisdom to know the difference."

I somehow became adept at informal public speaking by participating in the women's circle groups at church. The same lesson was reinforced when I found myself speaking before one of the groups, holding forth on some topic with great passion. As I concluded my presentation, a precious little lady came up to me, threw her arms around my neck and said, "Oh, Nelda, you were absolutely wonderful!" This compliment had the opposite effect from what was intended. Although I have always enjoyed praise, this time I clearly discerned a message: "Nelda, you have done this long enough. It's time for you to move on." I went home and told

Rex, "Honey, I will never give another church circle program."

GRADUATIONS

Shortly after that experience, I returned to school, getting an A.A. degree from Tallahassee Community College. I was then admitted to the College of Education at Florida State University and received my Bachelor's in elementary education degree from there in 1970 , graduating with honors at the age of 48! Since I had enrolled as a freshman at the age of 17, I often commented that it took me over 30 years to get that degree.

I had just graduated and was interviewing for teaching jobs in Tallahassee when Rex again received a promising offer; this time it was to join the faculty of the University of South Florida in Tampa. We decided we would return to Lakeland. I was delighted to be back in Lakeland. The three older children were in college and our youngest was a high school sophomore. Shortly after moving, I was hired as a fourth grade teacher in a fairly new school near our home, the site of several of my stories.

Those teaching days were happy and exciting. As I think about what influenced my success, I am convinced that love was the answer. The love that "God is" had always been flowing toward me. My husband, my family, my neighbors and friends, all were caring and affectionate toward me. (If anyone had ever rejected me or treated me unkindly, I had somehow succeeded in not experiencing it as such.) This wonderful support surely enabled me to be more accepting of others.

I had another boost, as well. Although I had never seen myself as "smart," during those early teaching years I completed a Master's program at the University of South Florida in Educational Administration and Supervision.

OPEN SPACE

After a few years of teaching fourth grade, I was asked to join the faculty of Scott Lake Elementary, a new open -space school, the first of its design in the district. It was very interesting to me to take part in that experiment. My participation enabled me to discover a wonderful truth: when a group of dedicated people are passionate about success, they will make it happen. To a person we staff members became imbued with high purpose; we felt we were on a mission.

Teaching in a classroom without walls was very different from my former experiences. The school was really and truly open. People were constantly walking through our spaces – teachers, parents, supervisors. We were often asked, "How in the world can you teach with all that noise?" Two things made it work. First, we had a great principal, who knew what he was doing. His philosophy was to let teachers alone to do their jobs. He gave us plenty of room to be creative and supported us all the way.

The second factor was the system of teaching we used; or at least, I did. There was no single stream of knowledge consisting of bits of wisdom being dispensed by the teacher alone. In our classrooms the stream went both ways; the students were the teachers as well as the faculty. There was much joy, much work and much success. I loved it, and the children did too. I stayed at Scott Lake for eight years.

VOLUNTEERS

One day Rex told me of a new position opening in the district office for a supervisor of the school volunteer program. They wanted someone who could develop and implement a new program. This appealed to me, but I was saddened at the thought of leaving the children. What would they do without me? (I was quite sure that I was absolutely essential in their lives.) The upshot was that I applied and was hired.

Working out of a district office was a challenge, and at first I was depressed. My "office" was an old army barracks building with no doors or privacy. Whereas I had just come from being part of a dedicated team that pulled together, everyone around me now seemed to have a different slant on things. There had been some scattered efforts at providing volunteers in some schools, but nothing had been coordinated. It was mine to do.

A major part of my job was influencing principals to permit school volunteers to become an integral part of their staffing. My message was that instead of being outsiders coming in to check on how well the school was doing (the fear of the administrators), the volunteers were highly motivated people who were there to focus their love and creativity on student learning. I'm very proud of the work we did in that position. When I started the job in 1976 there were 105 schools in Polk County and only a handful of volunteers. By the time I retired in 1984 we had placed volunteers in over 100 of those schools.

THE NEW GROUND

When I was a little girl, my father used to take my sister, my brother and me to a place we called the New Ground. It was additional land, which my father had purchased, cleared and tilled for the first time. In the middle of this patch of land was a sinkhole where huge wild grapevines grew. We kids used to hold on to the vines and swing through the air for what seemed very long distances.

As I look back to that experience, the New Ground seems to represent a theme in my life. It's a metaphor for swinging from one situation to another with trust, joy and abandonment. At various times in my life I've swung this way from one thing to another, doing the next thing I was supposed to do, seldom realizing that the changes represented transitions or passages.

One day while I was serving in the Polk County supervisory position, a bulletin crossed my desk announcing a course being offered in Orlando: Dr. Thomas Gordon's Effectiveness Training. I knew little about Gordon's model, but I took the announcement home and showed it to Rex. I had long since learned to trust my husband's sense of timing and his way of encouraging me toward key steps in my growth. He advised me to request that the district sponsor my attendance at this training. Recognizing that the communication skills offered in the course would benefit me in my job, my boss approved my proposal. I was about to swing over into new ground again. I have not been the same since.

TEACHER EFFECTIVENESS TRAINING

It is impossible to share in these pages all that I learned in that week of Teacher Effectiveness Training (TET), the teacher version of Gordon's famous Parent Effectiveness Training (PET). The course focused on relationships – how to get along with others, how to confront when you are experiencing problems, how to help others when they are having problems.

Back at my job with the Polk County school volunteer program, I put the Effectiveness Training skills to work. I began to listen better to others. My influencing was enhanced. I could get my needs met on the job. As I worked at mastering these skills, their effect on my work and other relationships was profound.

I soon found myself working with a variety of community groups. I often recruited their members as volunteers, then trained and assigned them to work in the schools with students, teachers and parents. In this effort, again the Gordon model proved invaluable. No two schools were alike and every principal was unique, so each school I visited was New Ground for me.

TEACHER TRAINING

After attending the TET trainer course to learn how to teach these valuable "people skills" to others, I began facilitating graduate courses for teachers sponsored by the Teacher Education Institute of Winter Park, Florida. Over the next several years I led TET classes from Austin, Texas, to Long Island, New York, and traveled all over Florida offering staff development programs to school personnel and volunteers. As it all came together, I had the strong sense that I had found my life's work. I retired from the school system and began to devote all of my time and energy to instructing the teacher courses.

One summer as I was teaching in Lynchburg, Virginia, I told the group that my next class was scheduled for Long Island. Their Southerner perceptions of Long Islanders were evident as they cautioned, "Oh, Nelda, don't go there. They'll eat you alive!" A week later, after the ensuing class was finished, I boarded the flight home carrying a dozen yellow roses, a token of the Long Island teachers' appreciation of my efforts. That turned out to be

the first of many trips I made to conduct classes there.

GRANDMOTHERHOOD

After my careers as teacher, volunteer supervisor and teacher trainer, I found another opportunity to make a difference with children through substitute teaching. Substituting was an enjoyable challenge. When you walk in as a new sub, you have no idea what you're getting into. A few years ago I accepted a call to substitute-teach a large group of students, a combined class of fourth and fifth graders. After a hectic morning, physical education time came. "Good!" I thought, "This will give me time to get myself together."

I walked out onto the playground and approached a couple of teachers who were standing there. They looked familiar to me. Then I recalled that they'd been in one of the graduate courses I'd taught in Lakeland in former years.

"Oh, Nelda," one of them said, "Do you know what we remember about you?"

"So?"

"One day in class you told us your first grandson had just been born." (Matt, the grandson, had just turned 16, so I realized how long ago that had been.) "You came back to class after spending some time with him and told us how precious he was to you. Then you said, 'I hope that every time you step into your classroom you will look at those children and think that one of them could be a Matthew.'"

The other teacher spoke up. "We've never forgotten that. To this day, when I look at one of my students, I think, 'That could be Matthew.'"

That incident spoke to me. It said, *You are supposed to be in this business. You know how to help people. Not teach them how to teach, but assist them in becoming better teachers. One way is to share your personal life with others.*

These days my wonderful Matthew is a college sophomore. I have pictures of me holding him when he was a baby. I'm quite sure it's one of the pictures I took to class and shared with those teachers as I told them how much I adored my first grandchild.

Jessica, my only granddaughter, has just graduated from high school. Grandson Taylor is a high school sophomore. Carlos, my foster grandson, is out of school and working in his father's business. I adore each one of them along with Matthew.

As a grandmother, I am grateful for the opportunity to apply what I've learned about uniqueness, attention, acceptance, love and caring, and affirmation in my relationships with each of them.

FURTHER CHALLENGES

In childhood times, my New Ground had always meant enjoyment. But change, inevitable in any life, can also bring difficulty and challenge. Three years ago I suffered severe vision loss, due to macular degeneration, and since then have had to pull in my wings. I am no longer able to drive or even to travel unaccompanied. Though I miss those exciting teacher-training times, my response to this life-changing event has been, as always, to move on. There is the writing of this book, the making of tapes, which Rex faithfully transcribes. I even had Jim Ballard, who instructed the first TET class I attended, as my writing coach.

My skills and experiences are coming into play in a new endeavor, my role as a life coach. Rex and I have both completed a two-year training program with Coach University, and are now involved in coaching clients. This is proving to be another area in which I use Dr. Gordon's communication and problem-solving skills to assist others to move on in their life and work.

As I continue to learn to cope with loss of my vision, I realize that the "little seamster" Mrs. Coomer recognized so many years ago is still in operation. She just keeps going on, going on.

SUMMARY

I have had the wonderful experience of being a successful teacher of students and of adults. Now that I have reached the age of 80, I have been piecing together the parts of my life that may have made that possible. As you read the stories about my students and the stories about who this Nelda is, you will see how my life has influenced my work and the contributions I have made to the lives of others and the contributions they have made to my life.

Writing this book has connected me to my reason for being. It is with a great amount of pride that I tell these stories and say all the things that I have said. I have again moved to new ground. I am still the "little seamster" that Mrs. Coomer described and I am glad.

My wish is that other teachers reading this book will reflect on their own success and joy in their work and in building relationships with students. In our world, sharing stories has become an important way to pass on our experiences. Stories can allow us to to know each other and value each other. If we all stay encased in our own being and do not reach out, our experiences will be lost. Stories are not important to teach or to fix others but to share so that others might learn from these experiences. It is one way we can connect in the world and make it better.

As you have read my stories about teaching, hopefully you have been awakened to the call of the teacher within you, the voice that calls you to honor your own true self. Listening to your inner teacher offers you the needed authenticity for coping with your own life forces, as well as the authority for creating positive relationships with children.

I hope all who read this book will be inspired to tell your stories. All of you have them!

We pay a heavy price for our fear of failure.

It is a powerful obstacle to growth, It assures the progressive

Narrowing of the personality and prevents exploration.

There is no learning without some difficulty and fumbling.

If you want to keep on learning, you must keep on risking failure --

all your life

-- John W. Gardner

ENDORSEMENTS

Given today's context of pressure for improved test scores, school violence and terror in our country, Nelda Toothman's <u>The Teacher Within</u> is just-in-time reading. This book reminds us of the importance of caring for every precious human being we encounter and how we can make a difference in the lives of others. Through sharing her stories, Nelda moves each of us to dig deep within and find what we are really made of. She inspires us to think about how we will behave given the challenges we face individually, in classrooms and in our Nation. A clear and compelling read that moves us through stories of a simpler time to great insights about ourselves and our humanness. Should be required reading for teachers, parents and for all those who wish to get in touch with their reason for being.

Dr. Marilyn Katzenmeyer
Teacher, Educational Consultant, Co-author, "Awakening the Sleeping Giant: Helping Teachers Develop as Leaders," 2nd Edition, Corwin Press, 2000.

In these uncertain times, we are searching for deeper connectivity to those in our world with whom we go about our routines. And that's what Nelda's book is all about. She takes us by the hand and shows us how to discover meaning in our daily, dutiful relationships and to find in them the wonder that transcends the obvious.

Rhea Chiles
Former Florida First Lady

_____

Nelda Toothman's stories are just like she is-- captivating, charming and always with a lesson. She'll bring you to laughter and to tears recounting many of the children she's touched or been touched by over the years. She'll also delight you with her honesty and simplicity. Most of all, Nelda will inspire every former, current or future educator to appreciate why one chooses the profession in the first place: the pure excitement and joy of teaching and learning with children.

Dr. Jim Croteau
Leon County Schools
Tallahassee, Florida

An inspiring statement from a dedicated teacher who really knew what schooling was all about!

J. Foster Watkins
Professor of Educational Leadership
University of Alabama at Birmingham

President Emeritus
Gainesville College
University System of Georgia

Nelda Toothman is most perceptive and loving. Her stories tell a little about who she is as a teacher and more about who we should all strive to become as human beings.

Sharon Benner
Assistant Superintendent
School District of Lee County
Ft. Myers, FL

Once again, Nelda's generosity of spirit and warm, welcoming ways shine through the stories of her life to compel us to be the same for others.

Maggie Wheeler
Coordinator of Community Involvement
Polk County (FL) School District

Within these vignettes and anecdotes are the buried treasures of a classroom teacher. Reading this caused poignant personal reflection. A must-read for every veteran teacher to help us remember why we do what we do. And new teachers will gain insight into the heart of what they are learning to do.

Dr. Merrie Lynn Parker
School Improvement Specialist
Academic Division
Manatee County (FL) School District

Sharing with Nelda Toothman her deep appreciation of what she has received and learned from diverse people, especially the children she has taught and truly loved, is an emotional and spiritual experience. Her stories reveal what she calls the magic of her life--the wonders of God's gifts of love bestowed in mysterious and unique ways among us all. Nelda's storytelling gently urges us to recall and share stories of our own.

William R. Snyder, Ph.D.
Department of Educational Leadership
Florida State University

Listen to the stories of a gifted teacher! Notice how her love of children transcends every thought and action. Join with me in feeling blessed and renewed by hearing her stories. Grace happens.

William H. Drummond
Professor Emeritus
University of Florida

From her first days of teaching from 1942 until now, Nelda inspires teachers to teach from their unique essence. Her vignettes sparkle with practical advice and touching humor in a true Southern storytelling style. Nelda has wrapped sixty years of wisdom into one fine book!

Cathy DeForest, Ph.D.
Educational Consultant

Printed in the United States
by Baker & Taylor Publisher Services